Playing Darlene

The True Double Life of a Public School Teacher & Professional Dominatrix

by
Darlene

Chances Press
www.chancespress.com

Playing Darlene is based on one woman's true life story. As such, the names of individuals and places may have been changed to protect the privacy of those involved.

TABLE OF CONTENTS

The Beginning

April 28, 2007 was Darlene's last day of work, or should I say "play?"

Darlene came into existence in the fall of 1990, but she was in my head when I was a child.

Perhaps I should start there.

Pasadena, California -- a quiet suburb near Los Angeles. Our house was in a "Leave It To Beaver" neighborhood, in which nice young ladies were limited in their pursuit of hobbies. Piano, violin, and ballet lessons were my choices. Since I preferred moving to sitting still, I opted for the latter, and when I was about seven, my mother started taking me to class. I liked it. I did well, and I got attention. Positive attention, not the constant negative feedback from her. (I was too short, my rib cage was too big, my forehead was too high, and I had the wrong color eyes). The people who watched me dance would tell me I was pretty and graceful. I loved moving to the music. It was sensual and made me feel alive inside. Not like at "home" where there was no touching and no emotion. Oh, wait. There *was* fear there. Plenty of that.

About the fear -- I was in a constant his state of fear because I never knew what my brother, who was three years older than I, would try to do to torture me next. My brother was in charge of everything, not my parents, and my father wasn't around very much. My father worked all night and slept all day. I hardly ever saw him, so my mother was the only available parent, but she didn't know how to be one. It was as if she were my brother's personal slave. She did whatever he told her to do. He was the real parent, and she was the child. And he was a tyrant. From about the age of eight onward, he would lie on the sofa in the living room and holler orders to her in the kitchen. "Bring me this, bring me that, bring me a Coke," and she would scurry around like a scared rabbit waiting on him hand and foot. I don't know why she was so afraid of him. What did he have on her? So, I never knew what he would do next.

He seemed to be obsessed with interfering with my life. He would find my homework and rip it up. Then I would have to go to school and make up some excuse to tell the teacher. I couldn't tell the teacher the truth -- that my brother had torn it to shreds, and my mother had done nothing about it.   I had to say something more believable, like the dog chewed it up. My mother was no help at all. ("Helpless" was her middle name). She didn't come up with any explanations for the teacher. It was up to me to come up with some story. And to make things worse, she was never angry with my brother for anything he did. It was always *my* fault. She'd say, as if reciting a lesson I had yet to learn, "It's your own fault. You are the one who made him mad at you." When it came to taking me to dancing lessons, my brother would interfere with that, too. He would get in the car and lock all the doors so that my mother couldn't get in. I'd be standing outside the car screaming at her, "Why don't you *do* something? Why don't you *stop* him?" Then she'd go into her "helpless" routine and say, "Well, there's nothing *I* can do. *You're* the one who made him mad at you. You have to learn."

Somehow baton twirling got itself added to the list of permissible activities, and after a while I became good enough at it to start competing in contests. My brother was once again on top of the situation. He would take my batons on the morning of the contest so that I couldn't go. He would stare right at me and, holding my baton case, calmly inform me that I didn't deserve to go. As a result, my baton teacher started keeping the batons, along with my costumes, at her house. She would pick me up and take me to the contest. This lady was going through all of this -- going to all this extra trouble because of my brother. I know she knew there was something very sick going on inside my house, but back then no one did anything about it. She must have thought it was completely unacceptable that my mother never did anything about him. I mean, my mother was *supposed* to be the parent, and my brother was all of 12 or 13 years old, so why was *he* running everything? One thing that made it possible was that he was home *all* the time. No, he didn't go to school. He finished the sixth grade and simply refused to go anymore. And no, my mother did nothing about that either. All of the above happened while I was in still in elementary school.

When I got into junior high and all during high school, I started having to leave my books and clothes at a friend's house so that my brother couldn't get to them. When I was a senior in high school, I was one of the group of girls who danced at the football games. We had these cute little outfits that we would wear, and I had to leave the entire costume, including the shoes, socks, and gloves, at a girlfriend's house so that my brother couldn't tear them up and prevent me from going to the football game.

And then there was the high school prom. I got a beautiful dress and shoes and had to leave everything at my friend's house. Sure enough, on the afternoon of the prom my brother was running around the house looking in all the closets for my prom dress. He had a knife in his hands and said he was going to shred it. He couldn't find it, of course, and it made him even angrier that I had outsmarted him. It felt to me as if I were in a prisoner-of-war camp, and the whole time my mother did nothing to protect me. She consistently blamed me for everything he did to me.

So about the fear -- it was constant. It was never safe to go to sleep. I'd fall asleep at school because I had been awake all night. I remember once in elementary school my mother came home from a conference with the teacher and was angry with me. "The teacher says you're falling asleep at school. What's wrong with you?" I couldn't believe she asked me that. I thought, "Well, you *know* what's wrong with me. I'm awake all night because it's not safe to sleep here."

This nightmare of a childhood had physical effects. I had stomach problems. You see, sometimes when I had to go to the bathroom, my brother wouldn't let me. I had to literally hold everything for hours. I couldn't go to a neighbor's house to ask to use the bathroom because my mother would say, "Oh, the neighbors will wonder what's wrong with our plumbing." Of course, I couldn't break the code of silence and tell them that my brother wouldn't *allow* me to go to the bathroom and his own mother did nothing to stop him.

When I was about fourteen, I started getting sick soon after eating. I'd have horrible stomach cramps. This was a problem at school because after lunch, I'd have to ask the teacher to go to the bathroom, and then I'd be in there for a long time -- I mean maybe an hour. It kept happening, so the school had to contact my "mother," who now *had* to take me to the doctor because the school wanted an explanation. I was right there when the doctor confronted my mother. "Mrs. *****, your daughter is only fourteen years old and she's developing a duodenal ulcer. What's going on at home?" My mother went into her "stupid" routine and responded with, "Everything's fine at home. I have no idea why she's so nervous all the time." And that was the end of it.

To this day I have to take medications for digestive problems, and when it comes to sleeping, I *always*, I mean always, sleep with the light on.

Back to when I was seven -- So there I was, onstage under the lights, dancing to the beautiful music and feeling pretty. I also felt the power. I couldn't see the faces of the audience, but I could tell when they weren't moving. They weren't whispering to one another. They weren't blinking. And at times, it seemed as if they had even stopped breathing. That's the power. I learned what to do to get it when I was 7, and from then on, I lived for it.

I started the baton lessons at the age of ten. For school events and talent shows, I was either dancing or twirling a baton. My days were filled with, lessons, rehearsals, and performances (in addition to school). I'd be a nervous wreck because of what was going on at home (real life), but my mother would say, "Don't think about that. Just put on a good show." (fantasy life) I became an expert at turning my emotions on and off. Mostly off.

By that time, I knew who I wanted to be when I grew up. I had watched enough movies and looked at enough fan magazines. Viva Las Vegas had just come out, and Ann-Margret was the lady every man wanted, in a fantasy at least. What was it about Ann-Margret? She looked like the fresh-faced girl-next-door, but then in the scene where she danced onstage with Elvis, she was making some moves that, a few years earlier, had prevented Elvis from being shown from the waist down on *The Ed Sullivan Show*. Hmm. On top of that, she rode a *motorcycle*. (Everyone knows only bad girls ride motorcycles). And one more confusing piece of evidence: She did a film called *Kitten With a Whip*. What in the world does *that* mean? A kitten is absolutely adorable and appears to be completely helpless.   It wants to be cuddled. But, this kitten had a *whip*? Why? To stop someone from getting too close? To prevent someone from giving the kitten the nurturing it seemed to be pleading for with those huge eyes? Hmm again. Ann-Margret was an enigma, and I wanted to be one too.

The next year, when I was eleven, I had my first opportunity when I twirled a baton in the school talent show. The baton was within a hoop to which fringe was attached. I would twirl the baton, some lights were turned off and others were turned on, and the audience wouldn't see me or the baton, only the hoop spinning magically by itself. The number was called, appropriately, "Hoop Fantasy." Here's the best part: the music my baton teacher had chosen was David Rose's "The Stripper." Yes, *that one*, with all the bumps and grinds. My mother and baton teacher would give each other amused looks because they thought they knew what was going on and I didn't. I was only eleven.

I knew.

And I loved it. This was not a G-rated number I was doing. I was a pre-teen sex object. No pretense. That was the clear intention. I wanted the boys in the audience to have "accidents" in their pants and the male teachers to fantasize about me later as I sat in their classes.

For the rest of junior high and high school, I danced at the school football games (in very short skirts) and in the school musicals. Jean MacLaren in *Brigadoon* and Dream Laurey in *Oklahoma* were my two favorite roles. In the latter, I got to dance with the "man of my dreams," a waltz, which is to this day, my favorite of all of the ballroom dances.

Then came college. By this time, I had gotten a job as a cashier in a market and escaped from "home" and its twisted inhabitants. I had survived my childhood and now had complete control over the rest of my life. Since I didn't know what to choose as a major, but had liked the typing and shorthand classes in high school, the counselor decided it should be business. I took all of the college level courses -- mathematical analysis for business, economics, and accounting. But the only classes I really liked were the ballroom dancing classes. The teacher was nice and let me attend more than just the one in which I was enrolled, so I think I spent about five hours a day in them. I learned the waltz, foxtrot, rumba, cha-cha, tango, East Coast Swing, and West Coast Swing. Each dance has a different attitude, so I could play a different part with each one. I moved well because of my ballet background, added enough of what I had learned as an eleven year-old, and made all of the men who weren't dancing with me wish that they were. Sometimes I tried to catch sight of their eyes to see exactly what they were looking at -- my face, hair, cleavage, derrière, or legs. I don't think it mattered what dance I was doing. Most of the men couldn't tell the difference between a waltz and a cha-cha anyhow. Visually, I helped all of this along by wearing short skirts and high heels. They were watching that, while my mind was somewhere else. I was connecting to the music and lost in my own fantasies.

I was floating and they were drooling, for *me* now, not Ann-Margret.

I ended up with a Bachelor's Degree in some useless thing, not business after all, and was still working in the grocery store. I had a lot of different jobs after that, some of them slightly impressive. For example, I was a computer programmer, complete with my own office and secretary, and I wasn't yet twenty-five. I hated it. It was fun learning the programming languages, but to actually sit in an office and do the job forty hours a week was depressing. Inside my mind, I was a dancer. I wanted to be out there in front of an audience showing the crowds what they wanted to see. Well, not literally. *Not yet anyhow.*

After the programming, I was a waitress at a Bob's Big Boy. It was the only waitressing job I could get since I had no experience, and they provided three whole days' worth of training. Even though most people would probably prefer relaxing behind a desk in a high-rise to schlepping burgers and fries, I much preferred life at the diner. I wore a costume -- okay, a uniform -- and it felt like I was in the entertainment business again. I had an audience, and the better my performance, the larger the tip. Ah, the tip. There was something about picking up the cash that had been left on the table. It wasn't applause, but I took it as a sign of approval. A paycheck at the end of the week just didn't excite me. After a few months though, I was bored. I wanted a new part to play, so I became a bank teller. Then an accounting clerk at the *Los Angeles Times.* That didn't last long because there I was, sitting in an office again.

I ended up returning to a grocery store because it paid well enough and offered flexible hours. Flexible hours meant I had time to go to dance classes day, evening or weekend again. But now I wanted a bigger audience than I got at the dances. I wanted to be on stage again.

I started going to auditions at community and dinner theaters. I got to dance in several musicals and was sometimes given solos, but I was usually cast as a girl-next-door type. I wanted to be eleven again. Remember "The Stripper?"

But by this time, I was in my late twenties. The life of a dancer is short. If I wanted to stay in any kind of show business, I would have to get up the nerve to talk. No music, no dancing, but at least I'd be in front of an audience and be able to feel the power that I'd felt when I was a child -- when I knew they couldn't take their eyes off of me.

For the next few years, I acted in a variety of theaters in the area. Nothing major. I loved the whole set up. The audience just sat there, and I created an unreal world for their entertainment. It didn't matter whether I was dancing or talking. I was the one performing the magic. I controlled *them*.

The problem then became the parts in which I was cast. I had blonde hair and blue eyes, but I had outgrown my girl-next-door type and was now the *mom* of the kid next door. Me, a *mom*? No.

Hell, no.

Also, I didn't get enough work in those roles to make ends meet. And I was getting tired of being almost broke, of being a waitress in some crummy eatery, and of renting a room in a broken-down house complete with rats and roaches.

I got depressed. I started going to twelve step meetings. Not for alcohol or other drugs, but one for children of dysfunctional families. Maybe that would help me understand and fix my so-far unfulfilling life. Once there I was sitting next to a lady I'd seen in several meetings. I'd enjoyed and related to much of what she had shared in the past. We started talking.

"What do you do?" she asked.

"Nothing right now. I'm trying to figure out what to try next," was my answer.

"You sound well-educated. Do you have a degree?"

"Yes, but it's worthless. It's in blah-blah-blah."

"Well, it qualifies you to do what I do. I teach English to immigrants." I thought that sounded very, very boring. She probably had half a dozen students in a church basement somewhere. She went on to tell me that she worked for the ____ ________ Unified School District and quoted me her hourly rate of pay.

"WHAT?! They pay you WHAT?"

"And you qualify," she assured me.

I told her I wasn't the teacher type. She said, "It's not like that."

I told her I had no patience with kids. She said, "They're adults."

I said a couple of other negative things about what I thought the job was and why I wasn't right for it.

She finally said, "Look. It's not like anything you've already seen. Come sit in my class."

I went. I saw.

It wasn't like anything I'd already seen. It wasn't like school. It wasn't like teaching.

It was *performing*.

So, I had to take a state exam and apply for a credential, but that was easy. I now felt I had a viable career. I could be in front of an audience again and earn enough to even have my own apartment. No more creature-infested rooms on the wrong side of town.

I was high on life. I felt good about myself. I had a career, not just a job. I had a nice apartment. I mean really nice. The students were wonderful, and since they were adults, I could talk to them as if they were neighbors. Some were college graduates in their own countries. To this day, a few are still friends.

The euphoria only lasted a couple of years. The students loved me, but I never got the feeling that any of the men were drooling. Ann-Margret was sexy at every age. Why couldn't I be?

I didn't want to stop teaching, but I had to figure out a way to add what was missing. The sexual side of me had been dormant for too long.

Since I believe that there are no accidents in life, it's not surprising that one day I happened to notice among the newspaper racks a paper that had a scantily-clad young lady on the front page. Of course, I took one to see what was inside it. It was full of ads for private dancing, massage, bachelor parties, escorts, lingerie shows, fantasies, fetishes, and things I'd never heard of. I wanted to somehow get involved in something, but I had no idea where to start. And these things were totally beyond anything I'd done in the past. I mean I had studied ballet and ballroom dancing, and acted in legitimate theater. Were the activities in this newspaper even legal? I couldn't risk getting arrested and losing my teaching credential.

I finally called a place of business that offered private, nude dancing. When I got there I saw it was a real business, not someone's house. It had been there for many years, which proved to me that whatever was going on in there was legal and, therefore, safe for me to do. I was nervous all right, but curiosity won out. I went in and saw a handful of young ladies lounging around in various states of undress. I asked the slimy (too much grease in his hair, rumpled clothing, and he badly needed a bath) guy behind the desk what I had to know how to do in order to work there. He looked at me as if I were crazy. I still looked like a soccer mom. He said something like, "This isn't the place for you." He was right. I don't know how to describe the "type" the girls were, but I wasn't it.

But I wanted very much to *be* that type. To *play* that type. I told the guy I was a dancer, looked great when dressed/undressed the way the girls were, and really wanted to try it. He sort of rolled his eyes, but finally told me to come in at noon the next day.

I showed up with my "costume" in a bag: a lacy bra, g-string, hot pants, and spike heels. I got dressed and positioned myself on one of the sofas in the lounge. When Mr. Slime saw me, I could tell from the look on his face that he was thinking this may work out after all...

He then explained the way things worked. Some guy would just walk in off the street, look around at the girls, and choose me. I was to take him to one of the rooms and pull the curtain across the doorway. (There were no doors). I could dance around and take off some or all of my clothes, but I wasn't allowed to touch him. He could touch himself, and there was a bottle of oil provided for this. The first time I was selected, I felt a twinge of panic. I was used to performing dances that had been choreographed and well-rehearsed. No one had ever taught me how to do a striptease on purpose.

Where was I supposed to look? Should I gaze into his eyes and smile? Should I pretend he isn't there? Or should I flat-out stare at his dick and wait for the explosion?

I worked there for a couple of months. I'd go in at noon, work/dance until five, change clothes, and teach my ESL class in the evening. I got a kick out of it. Now and then, one of my students would ask me something like, "Teacher, what did you do today?" They wouldn't have believed me if I had told them.

I didn't make much money with this dancing thing. There wasn't that much business. Most of the time I was just sitting around the lounge reading a magazine or talking to one of the ladies. What I preferred, though, was listening to them. They discussed other aspects of the sex industry that I knew nothing about.

Then one fateful day -- someone mentioned slaves, whips, chains, and dungeons. That sounded like some kind of theater (oh, good--acting again), and I wanted to know more about it. I heard the word "Castle", but that was it. The conversation was interrupted, and I didn't know where it was.

I went home that night and went through the phone book. There must have been dozens of businesses starting with the word "Castle". The Castle Liquor Store, The Castle Nursery School, and even The Castle Laundromat. I started calling. And calling. I was on a mission. "Is this the place with the whips and chains?" I'd say over and over again. "Sorry, lady, you've got the wrong number" was the usual response.

Finally, this place had to be in the phone book.

And it was. Finally a guy on the other end of the phone said in a slow drawl, "Yeah, we got that."

I went right over.

When I got there, I was pissed about what I saw. The slow guy must have given me the wrong address. There was no business there. There was just an old house. I was in a business district on a well-traveled street in Hollywood, but this old house was nothing. It didn't say anything on the building. It couldn't be a theater.

I parked anyhow and started walking around. Maybe I could ask someone. The place I was looking for was probably nearby. There were no people around to ask. I had to try *something*. I went to the door of the old house and knocked. Nothing. I decided to try the door, and it was unlocked. Who leaves a door unlocked in this town? I opened it and inside there was just a stairway. Still no people.

But I heard a voice. The voice of the guy with the slow drawl. Of course, I went up the stairs. There was the guy, sitting behind a desk and talking on the phone. He looked like an extra from an old episode of *Gunsmoke*: unshaven, clothes that looked as if they'd been slept in, and crooked, filthy teeth -

- what was left of them anyhow. Behind him on the wall there was a lot of what seemed to be equipment, but I didn't recognize anything except a pair of handcuffs. He gave me a blank stare.

"Can I help you?"

"I called a little while ago. You gave me the address, but I don't see...I mean I thought this was a kind of theater. What do you *do* here? I've done acting. What would I have to know to work here?"

"You got to talk to my mistress."

He called someone on the phone.

Out pranced a bubbly lady who introduced herself as Mistress Victoria. She appeared to be in her late thirties, had platinum hair, and reminded me of an actress who was popular in the sixties, Connie Stevens. I told her I wanted to ask about working there. She checked me out in detail. I mean everything -- my face, eyes, hair, makeup or lack thereof, clothing, hands, legs, even fingernails.

She asked, "Why do you want to work here? You're not in the scene."

"Scene?" I thought. I was an actress. I knew what scenes were.

That wasn't at all what she meant.

I asked her to tell me what the employees did there. She said that if I didn't know, it wasn't the place for me.

I said I *really* wanted to know.

She sounded exasperated when she said, "Okay, look. For an hour you're going to be in a room alone with a client. He'll order you to take off all your clothes. All of them. You'll be naked. Then he'll tell you to get on all fours. He'll put a collar around your neck and attach a leash to it. He'll further instruct you to crawl on the floor after him, like a dog, and bark on command. What are you going to do?"

I was thinking, "My God. She's *serious*," but what came out of my mouth was, "I could do that."

She said, "No, you couldn't. You're not into it."

"*I couldn't?*" I thought, outraged. This was a challenge I couldn't pass up. I went on to tell her I'd acted a wide variety of roles and was certain I could pull it off.

She finally agreed to let me try. She said it would take me a couple of days to get ready. I didn't know why until she took me into the "lounge" to meet the other ladies. Oh my gosh! What a cast of characters. White faces, purple lips, long black fingernails, pierced tongues, tattoos *everywhere*, and leather. Leather boots, leather skirts, leather bodices. Then a lady strolled through carrying a see-through bag containing, what else, a leather whip, leather paddle, and leather riding crop.

Not everyone was wearing leather. There were a few ladies who wore dresses/skirts made of satin or even velvet. But there was a harshness about all of them. No one smiled. No one really looked *normal*. I didn't know what kind of outfit would look right on me, but I told her I had gotten the idea.

It was Tuesday. She said to come in Friday at six. By then she'd have me on the schedule. "Oh, and what's your name?"

"Jane."

I immediately sensed that that was the wrong answer. "That's not your real name, is it?"

"Yes. Is there another Jane here?"

"Sweetie, you need a *name*. Who are you going to *be*?"

For the next two days I visited some places on Hollywood Boulevard that sold clothing like I had seen the ladies wearing, but bought nothing. Then I went to Santa Monica Boulevard. I still didn't have a clue as to who I *was* and felt I needed to do some research. I finally found an adult book/video store that didn't look the least bit sleazy from the outside. It looked safe and clean and you could even see through the floor-to-ceiling windows. When I walked in, I did notice that I was the only female in the place, but, oh well, I was already in. The clerk didn't seem to be fazed, and when he asked if he could help me, I came right out with it.

"I'm going to start working at The Castle and I want to become more familiar with what they do there."

I was relieved that I didn't have to answer any more questions. He knew *all* about it. He proudly showed me the S & M, the B & D, the fantasy, and the fetish sections -- and the subdivisions thereof: dominants, submissives, and switches.

The last category was further broken down into dominant switches and submissive switches. A switch is a lady who is willing to play either part, but usually leans one way or the other. A dominant switch would likely wear black leather, whereas a submissive switch would choose a typically feminine outfit.

I was lost and finally asked him to just pick a couple that would give me a general overview. I went home and watched them, but I really didn't see how I was going to be able to accomplish such a transformation after all. I couldn't figure out how to change my appearance enough to blend in with the rest of the group.

Then the epiphany.

I *wouldn't* change anything. I would be the one who looked different -- the one who looked as if she didn't belong there. I was raised in a polite, refined suburb that had a distinctly Southern feel: a slower pace of life, neighborhoods in which couples took after-dinner constitutionals, and front porches on which ladies would sit and enjoy sloe gin fizzes in the late afternoon.

That was it. I would be gracious and delicate. I would wear lingerie made of lace complete with an old-fashioned garter belt and stockings. Now I needed a typical Southern name.

I called The Castle and told the guy behind the desk (who turned out to be Mistress Victoria's personal slave) that I had decided on a name: Darlene.

He said, "You look like a Darlene," and went on to tell me that I had already been booked for an appointment on my first evening with "Uncle Bob."

I got there in plenty of time to get ready for my new family member. From head to toe, I was in white -- a white lace negligee definitely not concealing a white lace bra, white lace G-string, white lace garter belt, and white stockings. On my feet I wore white bedroom slippers, with spike heels. Oh, and in my hair was a white lace ribbon. I felt very confident about my outfit. It had been well-planned. But about my upcoming session, not at all. Yes, I had acted in lots of plays, but always with a script that I had memorized perfectly ahead of time. This role-playing business was new to me. I'd never done improvisation.

When I left the dressing room and started walking to the lounge to sit with the other ladies, the Mistress saw me. She just stared. I didn't know what she was going to say. For what must have been about fifteen seconds, apparently she didn't know what she was going to say.

She finally just shrugged her shoulders *as if* to say, "Oh well...who knows...it might work."

I hadn't been lounging for very long when I was called to the front desk to be introduced to my Uncle. He told me I looked lovely, but that he had brought an outfit for me to wear. He handed me a plain brown bag. I was told to go back to the dressing room, change (and wear *only* what was in the bag), and meet him in the dungeon that he had reserved for us.

I followed directions, unhappily removing my carefully-planned costume and replacing it with Bob's preference. I was disappointed to say the least. I didn't get it at all. There were just two articles of clothing in the bag, a tank top and shorts. No bra. No panties. No shoes. When I finished dressing, I caught a glimpse of myself in the mirror. I looked about 15 years old.

Got it.

At this point, let me explain what's supposed to happen. I meet with the client in one of the vacant rooms and for a few minutes we are to discuss what he has in mind. I had already been told that since I was new and didn't know anything about "the scene," I had to start as a submissive. Therefore, the client would be the dominant one. He might have a variety of interests. For example, does he want to tie me up? Spank me? Paddle or whip me? Torture me with ice or candle wax? Act out a scenario including any of the above? So, we are to talk about it and come to an agreement, in detail, as to what will happen in the session. Here's the part that was music to my ears: It's up to me to agree to his desires or not. I could say no to any or all of it. He would then have to interview another lady if I refused. If we did, in fact, decide on the activities, we would then go together to the front desk and sign up by saying something like, "We're going to play for forty-five minutes in the Citadel." (Each room had a different name -- the Tower, the Boudoir, the Chamber, and the Sanctuary).

After that, we'd pick up a mesh bag in which to carry whatever equipment we needed, such as handcuffs, wrist/ankle cuffs, blindfold, ball gag, etc. Next, we'd go into our chosen dungeon. When we were ready to start the session, it was up to me to push the button on the intercom, after which the desk person would say, "Thank you" and start the clock. When the time was up, there would be a beep on the intercom, and the desk person would listen for me to say either, "Thank you" or "We'd like to extend the time." If, however, during our playtime, the client tried to do *anything* not previously agreed to, it was up to me to continue or end the session. Thus, the man was only allowed to do what I had already given him permission to do. Oh, did I say that *he* was the dominant one?

This job was perfect for me. I had the power. I was seven years old and on the ballet stage all over again.

About an hour later, Uncle Bob and I had concluded our session, and I was once again in my virginal attire, sitting in the lounge with the other ladies. I saw two more clients that first evening. I had earned more than I had teaching school for four days, and I had only "worked" a total of one hour and forty-five minutes.

So began eighteen years worth of "sexual" encounters with men with whom I never had sex, for there was no touching (for the purpose of sexual arousal) allowed.

You're probably wondering what Uncle Bob did for that hour with his fifteen year old niece...

Uncle Bob

I had been a bad girl. I liked Uncle Bob and looked forward to spending my summers at his farm, away from the city where I lived with my parents. I could pretty much do whatever I liked -- go horseback riding, fish at the pond, or just hang out with the cows and chickens. He'd lived in his community for a long time, and his neighbors all knew and liked him. Every weekend he'd have a dance in his barn at which I'd met some of the local boys. They were pretty nice, and Uncle Bob approved of most of them. But, see, Uncle Bob had this one rule: I was not allowed to hitch a ride into town.

Since I was only fifteen, I guess I thought he wouldn't really expect me to be perfect, so I went and broke the rule *and* got caught. Now he was telling me that he was going to call my parents and send me back to the city for the rest of the summer. I couldn't believe it. This was the very first time I'd ever done it. Wasn't he going to give me another chance? Sorry. A deal was a deal.

I begged, pleaded, whined, and cried. Nothing was working. He just stared at me.

Finally I said, "Please, Uncle Bob. There must be *something* I can do to make up for it. Please. I'll do *anything*. Really!"

"Really?"

"Yes, yes, really. Whatever you say."

"Well, there is something...you'd have to endure my punishment, and you'd have to swear *never* to tell your parents."

"I promise, Uncle Bob. Cross my heart and hope to die."

He took me out to the shed (a designated corner of the room). He put me inside and told me to wait there until he came back. When he returned, he had some thin tree branches in his hand. He then told me to take off my shorts. I didn't move at first. I couldn't believe what was about to happen. He repeated his command. This time I knew he meant it, so I just did as I was told. He bent me over a table. For several seconds he did nothing, and I thought maybe he'd changed his mind. Then came the first swat. Yikes! I'd never even been spanked by my parents and these were dry branches. *And* I wasn't wearing any panties, remember? I started to cry immediately. After I'd been struck a few more times, I got the nerve to say, "Please stop Uncle Bob. I've learned my lesson."

"Not a chance. You have a lot more coming to you."

My crying got louder. Every time I was hit, I'd let out a louder yell. This went on for several more minutes.

Then he stopped. I thought he was finished, so I stood up straight, but it turned out he was only giving his arm a rest.

When he started in on me again, he had switched hands. Now I was desperate. I couldn't take it anymore. I began hollering as loudly as I could.

"I swear I'll *never* do it again, and I'll *never* tell my parents..." Then I backed away from the table and fell to the ground in a ball, my head over my knees.

He stopped. There was silence for the next few minutes during which I was afraid to move.

Finally he leaned the branches against a wall, told me to put my shorts on, and left the "shed." He sat down in a chair on the other side of the room.

I followed instructions and got dressed but didn't move beyond that. I had learned to do no more than exactly what I'd been told.

He continued to sit there and stare at me. I continued to stare at the ground.

Another ten or so minutes passed. Then I heard a beep. Oh, God, the *BEEP*. I was shocked back to reality and in a firm, adult (teacher) voice, I said loudly and clearly, "Thank you."

That was it. It was over. I picked up the bottle of rubbing alcohol and squirted the surfaces of the furniture we'd touched. I wiped off everything with the towels I'd been told to bring in. I was then supposed to go *with* my client to the front desk where he would pay for the session. But Uncle Bob had one more surprise for me. As I was walking toward the door of our room, he pressed some cash in my hand. I didn't look at it. I just put it in the pocket of what were now *my* shorts. I felt very, very proud.

At this point, my life looked like this: Monday through Thursday I taught school, and Friday through Sunday I played at the Castle. And I absolutely *loved* the combination. I was acting in two different plays and the roles couldn't have been more dissimilar. Just when I'd get bored with pretending to be the "good" girl, it would be time to make believe I was the "bad" girl. Which was the real me? I was much too busy to think about that.

Ed

Let me tell you about Ed. Apparently, he had been a client for a long time. His session was as plain and simple as his appearance. Ed was about five foot four, clean shaven, and had a face as flat as a pancake. He was bald and wore wire-rimmed glasses. I imagined he was a bookkeeper. He didn't really walk -- he sort of *marched* in with his own equipment. He brought a heavy wooden paddle that he carried in brown paper grocery bag. Ed's session was so simple that the interview took less than a minute. *Really.* He wanted me to hit him with his wooden paddle. He would lie on the floor on his stomach, and all I had to do was whack him with it. And he liked it hard.

The reason he brought his own paddle was that he would be responsible for cleaning it. I was responsible for cleaning the equipment that was used in the session if the equipment belonged to the Castle, but Ed would have to clean his own paddle. That was good because Ed had hemorrhoids, very bad hemorrhoids. They would bleed, so by the end of the session there was a lot of blood all over his wooden paddle, but that was his problem. If he had allowed me to lay a towel over his rear end, the blood would have merely gotten all over the towel, but no. Ed needed to feel the heavy wooden paddle on his bare skin.

So, there he was, on his tummy on the floor and I was smacking him as hard as I could. Toward the end of the session he started to squirm around a little. He was really grinding against the floor and by doing that he was able to arouse himself. Eventually he got off doing that. I was paddling him, and he was making a mess on the towel that he had put beneath him on the floor. There was no talking, no explanation for doing what I was doing. He just wanted me to keep hitting him with that paddle. I always wondered what he was reliving or why he wanted to have this kind of session, but I never got any information out of him. This was probably the simplest session I ever did, as well as the one of the ones with the least conversation.

Road Trip to Vegas

My older brother and I are on a road trip to Vegas. He's twenty-one, and I'm sixteen. I'm wearing a tank top and shorts. I'm barefoot and my toe nails are painted bright red. He's driving, and I'm in the passenger seat with my feet up on the dashboard. We're listening to the radio. He's talking about all kinds of things -- football, cars, music, and stuff he does with the guys at college. I'm sort of listening while I sing along with the radio. I'm also keeping time to the music with my feet. I'm wearing shorts, remember, and my legs and feet are constantly moving around and distracting my brother from his driving. That's the whole point. My legs, feet, and bright red toe nails are *really* turning him on. But he's my brother and I'm only sixteen. Oh, and I'm munching on potato chips. That's also part of the scene.

I say I don't like the song that's being played right now and ask to change the station. He tells me to go ahead and change it, but I have to use my feet. I start pushing the buttons with my toes. I still can't find a station I like, so I start turning the dial with my toes. He's trying to drive, but he's really watching my feet as they play with the buttons and knobs on the radio. And the smell of potato chips... He starts driving with only one hand on the wheel because the other hand has moved to his crotch. He begins to rub his dick, but very cautiously so I won't notice. Of course, I don't notice anything. I'm busy singing along and looking out the window.

He's sure I'm not paying any attention to him, so he unzips his pants and reaches inside. He's actually stroking his cock as he's driving, and I start commenting on the vegetation -- Joshua trees, tumble weeds, and cacti. Now he's certain he can get away with everything, and he actually comes all over his pants. I see nothing, but I do smell something. I ask him if he smells something funny, and he says he doesn't smell anything, only the potato chips... The session ends before we get to Vegas.

Footnote: The client brought the tank top, shorts, potato chips, and radio with him. The red nail polish had been delivered the day prior to our session so that I would have plenty of time to paint my toenails. I got to keep everything but the radio.

The Do Gooders

I had been working at the dungeon for a couple of months when an interesting incident happened. There was a local group I'll call the Do Gooders who somehow got the idea that several illegal things were going on inside such as: ladies were engaging in sex, some were under the age of eighteen, ladies were being paid off in drugs, and a few were minors who had been "lured" there from a religious retreat for teenage runaways that was next door. On top of that, the Do Gooders claimed that the ladies and/or the clients were being tortured and their shrieks could be heard all the way inside the Catholic-run home.

One night I went to work for my usual shift (8 P.M. to 3 A.M.), and when I got there I noticed several young men in front of the building, picketing. They were walking in a circle around a parking meter. I didn't bother trying to read what

their signs said. I drove past them into the parking lot. I
ignored them and just walked in the building, figuring I would
hear about what was going on when I got inside.

Mistress Victoria waltzed triumphantly into the lounge and
announced to the ladies that the media were on their way.
Reporters from the three major networks wanted to interview
someone and she needed someone to volunteer to talk on
camera. "Dawn" couldn't do it because her grandfather would
have a heart attack. "Chloe" couldn't do it because her boy-
friend was under the impression she worked in a restaurant. I,
of course, couldn't do it because after all, I was a *credentialed
teacher*. No one wanted to be interrogated for the news. Then
I started thinking, 'What difference does it make that I'm a
schoolteacher? I teach four nights a week, and the other three
nights I'm here at the dungeon. One thing has nothing to do
with the other, and it's none of the school district's business
what I do in my spare time. Besides, who would be a better
defender of the Castle than I?'

I was a bit older than some of the ladies, (a good thing), I
was well spoken, and, because of my acting background, I
knew I wouldn't become flustered on camera by any of the
reporters' questions. For a minute I thought, "Oh my gosh -- I
could lose my credential." But the rebel in me spoke up. My
next thought was, "Just let them try."

I volunteered.

The reporters and camera crews had assembled just outside the front door. I went downstairs and stepped outside. I was met with bright lights blinding me and microphones being shoved in my face. I was asked what I thought of the accusations. I responded by saying that the Do Gooders should come in, have a free tour, and find out for themselves what really goes on inside. Then they would realize their claims were groundless, and they could leave and go on to fight real crime in the city. The "interrogation" couldn't have lasted more than a couple of minutes, and although I was scared that I wouldn't be able to think on my feet, I loved being treated like a celebrity.

The story was the first segment on the eleven o'clock news on all three major channels that Friday night. When I was on camera, at the bottom of the screen it said:

"Darlene"
Castle spokesperson
____ _________ Unified School District teacher

All weekend long I was thinking, "Oh God, I've done it now. Monday evening when I show up at school, the shit will hit the fan."

That following Monday I expected to at least be called into the principal's office, if not immediately fired. To my amazement, that didn't happen. In fact, nothing happened. *Nothing.* How was that possible? Didn't *anyone* who worked for the entire school district watch the eleven o'clock news? Or was it that no one recognized me? Or could it be that no one even cared? Looking back, I really believe it was the latter.

Anyhow, that was the end of that. The little band of young men picketing outside only lasted a couple of more days, during which time a local radio talk-show host devoted his whole program to this notorious frivolousness.

After a few days, everything was back to the usual. Actually, business was a lot better than usual. The publicity had increased the curiosity of the public, and the Castle was busier than it had ever been...

Mark

I ended up getting many new clients as a result of my fifteen seconds of fame. Mark, for example, came in specifically to see Darlene, the teacher. He had seen me on the news and wanted to meet whoever this woman was. We started our interview in one of the empty rooms, and I asked him what he wanted to do in the session.

He said, "I don't know. I don't know anything about this. I just wanted to meet you."

I told him that the way it worked was that we had to decide during the interview what we wanted to do in the session and then actually do a session. We couldn't just sit around and talk.

He said, "Okay, let's sign up so that I can talk to you for an hour."

So that's what we did. We took no equipment in the dungeon with us. We just started talking. He told me that when he saw the ladies in the lounge, they all looked kind of scary to him as if they were dressed for Halloween. I was the only normal looking one there. He asked me what I was doing there and why I wanted to work there. I didn't going to any depth. I just said that I had a background in acting, and I thought it would be fun to work here. Then he started asking me very ordinary date-type questions such as, "Where did you go to high school?" and, "What's your favorite movie?" Then he said, "If you weren't here, you'd probably be out somewhere on a date. Where would you probably be having dinner?" That whole hour was just more of this first-date type of conversation. He admitted that I'm exactly the type of lady he would have wanted to date in college. I was flattered and thought this was very weird because he was talking about normal daily life and here we were inside a building in which normal daily life never happened.

The world inside the Castle was completely unreal. Finally he asked me if he could really take me out on a date, and I told him that that was against the rules. He said he'd be back, and he certainly was. He came back a few weeks later for our second date. This time he asked me to choose some type of equipment to play with. He wanted me to show him some of the things we did there. I brought handcuffs, a blindfold, and a black leather riding crop into our session.

I told him to take off all his clothes. At first he was reluctant, but I said, "That's what we do here. It's legal, so *do* it." I put his hands behind his back and put the cuffs on him. I then put the blindfold on him and started to caress his body with the riding crop. I started with his back and went from his shoulders on down to his feet. Then I walked around to the front. I started to swat his nipples, and what do you know? He started getting an erection. So, of course, I worked my way down *there* with the crop and started tapping his cock with it. I guess he was kind of embarrassed about his response because he attempted to take my attention away from the obvious by engaging me in second-date types of questions: "So what was your major in college?" I mean *really*. The guy is blindfolded and handcuffed and I'm wearing Darlene's usual lacy lingerie including a garter belt, stockings, and high heels and he's talking as if we're just having a burger and fries. We were getting toward the end of our time, so I told him he had behaved well and now deserved a special treat.

I removed the handcuffs and put the bottle of oil in one hand. He still couldn't see and asked me what it was. When I told him, he didn't get it, so I took the bottle from him and dripped the oil all over his cock. I then said, "Congratulations. You've earned the right to entertain me."

He said, "Are you kidding? I can't do it in front of someone."

I pointed out that since he was blindfolded, he should just pretend that I wasn't there. "Go ahead. Try it. Let's see what happens. We're just playing, remember?"

He did as I suggested, and I put a hand towel in his spare hand so that he wouldn't come all over the carpet.

At one point he stopped and said, "Sorry. I can't do it."

I responded by saying, "Shut up. You have no choice," and gave his rear end a strong swat with the crop. Well, that was it. That's what did it for him. He came in the towel.

When I removed the blindfold, he had a scared look on his face. We had discovered something about him that he didn't even know, and it was like now he was afraid of the secret getting out. Only Darlene knew what really turned him on. That created a kind of intimate bond between us, which was weird because we really didn't know one another at all. I didn't know if his name was really what he had told the desk person, and he certainly didn't know my real name. Two strangers with a very personal secret.

That's how my relationship with Mark started. He continued to see me for the next eighteen years, during which time he married and had two children. We did exchange phone numbers and talked on the outside. He and his family have moved out of state, but to this day he calls me twice each year: at Christmas and on my birthday. I wonder what his wife would think if she knew that during her entire marriage, he had been having an "affair" with Darlene.

The Art of Spanking

This client's name was Art. At least, that's what he said it was, and his session was about the "art" of spanking. I don't think you could really make a college-level course out of it, but I do believe one could develop a certain level of skill through diligent practice.

So, here was Art, wanting to teach me all about it and to take me to my limit. I told him that I was a "light submissive" which meant that he couldn't hit me hard at all. He said he knew I could do better and he would show me how. I agreed to the session, knowing full well that he wasn't going to show me anything unless it was *my* idea. I'm in charge, *remember?*

We signed up at the front desk, and I grabbed a few towels from the laundry room. No equipment was necessary. We walked into the dungeon, I pushed the button on the intercom, and the desk person's voice responded with, "Thank you." We began what was known as a simple over-the-knee spanking session. He sat on the bondage table and spread a towel over his lap. Then he told me to remove my g-string. He pulled me over his legs. He raised up my lacy negligee and began patting my cheeks. It actually felt kind of nice. He had big warm hands.

But then the pats began to get a little harder. Just when I was about to tell him he was spanking me too hard, he stopped. He started to *massage* my derriere. This was very strange, I thought, but it also felt good. He rubbed and lightly caressed me for a couple of minutes. Then everything changed and he started spanking me again, only harder this time. I mean, I *knew* it was harder, but it didn't really hurt, so I didn't stop him. These swats gradually increased in intensity over the next few minutes, and again, just when I was on the verge of saying something, he stopped. "How did he know when to take a break? How could he possibly know?" I wondered to myself.

Once again, he started rubbing my cheeks. He said they were beautiful, very rosy. Oh, great. Now my ass was a work of art.

This spanking/massaging pattern continued for another fifteen minutes or so. Inevitably though, he did reach my limit. My rear end was finally beginning to feel sore, and frankly I was just plain tired of the whole thing. I used the magic words, "My Mistress." (The agreement is that if the lady says that, the client has to stop doing whatever he's doing). To stay in character, I actually said, "My mistress would want you to stop now, but thank you." I went on to say that I had found it very arousing as well as educational. Also, I told him I was glad he had chosen me as his "pupil." Apparently, he was happy. He tipped me forty dollars, didn't take off any of his clothes, and didn't play with the oil. Some did, some didn't. Easy session.

I never saw him again, probably because he always wanted a new student.

The JPL Gadget Guy

During my interview with this man, he immediately volunteered the information that he worked at the Jet Propulsion Lab in nearby Pasadena. Of course, he had no idea where I was from and never would have guessed that not only had I grown up there, I had dated a man who also worked there and had even been taken on a tour of the place. Small world. Anyhow, he took something out of his pocket and proudly showed it to me. It was a gadget that he had made himself, a ring that went around the base of his cock. There were two cords attached to it which were to be tied to the two rings at opposite ends of the suspension bar in the dungeon.

I needed no more explanation. Since he asked to be restrained, it went without saying that he also wanted to be teased to distraction. The good old "tie-and-tease" (one of my favorite types of sessions).

We entered the room, and I pushed the button on the intercom. The voice from the front desk said, "Thank you." The clock was now running. I looked at him intently for a few seconds. He just stood there waiting for me to do something. It was all up to me, just the way I liked it. I slowly walked toward him with a seductive look in my eyes. I got *very* close, touched his temple with my fingers and lightly ran them down his face, caressing his cheek. "You know why we're here," I purred in his ear. "Now take off your clothes."

He did so and folded them neatly on the bondage table. He had been well-trained.

I walked to the suspension bar, turned, and gave him a "come and get me" stare. "What are you doing over there, sweetie? Don't you *want* me?" He responded eagerly, but as he was just about to touch me, I stopped him. "Wait. Now wait right there." I got some rope from the wall and tied his hands behind his back. I wanted him to feel helpless even before I attached his little device. I picked up the thingamajig and dangled it in front of his face. "Look what I have here. Where do you think this might fit?" I let my eyes drop from his face, go slowly down his body, and stop at his cock. "Oh, look - I think it would go nicely right here." With that, I put the ring in place and tied the cords to the bar above him. I placed myself a few feet in front of him. "Now walk toward me, honey." He edged his way forward until the cords were taut, creating pressure at the base of his cock, which was already becoming erect. Then my fun really began.

There I was in my lacy red negligee, red bra, red g-string, red garter belt, red stockings, and red high heels armed only with a black riding crop. I stood just a short distance away. "Come on darling. I know you want to touch me. Try harder."

But he couldn't. There was already too much stress on his dick, and he could only make a few inches in progress. I tapped it with the crop in an attempt to tantalize him. He was annoyed. Or even more aroused. Or both. The poor thing. I moved closer to him and whispered in his ear. "You know, I think you're an extremely attractive gentleman." I got within inches of him and started to touch parts of his body. I lightly ran my fingers through his hair, down the back of his head, and then forward along his jaw. I outlined his eyebrows, nose, and lips. Ah, the lips. They're just so sensitive, aren't they? I was *so* close to him, and he was really straining to lessen the space between us, but too bad. My fingers made their way down to his chest, and, naturally, I couldn't pass up playing with his nipples just a bit. I squeezed them and tugged at them. I gently ran my fingernails over his tummy down to his navel and beyond, to that area I find so sexy, the place below it, that *almost* forbidden zone. I played with the hair beneath his bellybutton, on down to the base of his you-know-what.

When I reached the ring of his self-made gadget, I lifted my hands. I could hear a slight gasp, a little "Oh, no!" He had been anticipating feeling my delicate fingers on his cock. Too bad again. That wasn't allowed. I could only touch his private parts with equipment; therefore, back to the riding crop. I lightly swatted the head of his dick a few times. He started drooling, and I don't mean from his mouth. "Oh my, look what's happening. You really must control yourself."

I decided to take this torture to the next level, so I stood directly in front of him as closely as I could without touching him. Then I moved the straps of my negligee off my shoulders and allowed it to drop to the floor. He stared at my body and I knew what he was thinking. I knew what he wanted to do to me if only his mobility hadn't been so restricted. "This could only get better," I thought, so I unhooked my bra and held it in place with one hand while I slid the bra straps off my shoulders with the other. He was expecting me to let the bra fall, so, needless to say, I didn't let it. I held it there and walked behind him. Then I took the bra and threw it on the floor in front of him. How frustrating for this pitiful man. He could see it but not the luscious breasts that used to fill its lacy cups. I decided to let him at least feel what he couldn't see, so I reached around his waist from behind and pressed my breasts into his back. This elicited a larger gasp. The drooling, by the way, had increased. (I had already placed a towel on the floor in front of him - the usual procedure).

Finally, I said, "Look. The only way I'm going to let you go is if you entertain me, but I'll only give you a minute, no more."

He was ready and willing, and confidently stated, "Yes, please mistress. I'm sure I can do it."

I untied his hands and moved in front of him, holding the crop. At last he could see my 36D breasts. "Go. The clock is ticking." He started stroking and staring, stroking and staring. The seconds were passing. I added to the pressure by saying, "You're time is almost up."

At that point he begged, "Mistress, may I come?"

"Look at me." I wanted to see desperation in his eyes. I gave him a stern look and waited a few seconds. I wanted him to panic a little and think, "Oh God. What if she doesn't *let* me come? What am I going to do?"

But that would have been too cruel. So, I let my eyes smile at his and softly said, "Yes, you may."

And he did, just in time.

He let me keep his invention, which I ran through the washing machine and went on to use on other clients.

The Strip Club

I'd been working/playing at the Castle for about a year when a couple of the ladies made a suggestion. They also danced at a strip club, and one day they asked if I'd like to come dance with them. They were barely twenty-one, and I was in my early thirties. I felt comfortable being nude in front of one client at a time, but to be nude on a stage and in front of a whole room of men? I didn't think I'd have the nerve to do *that*. I told them I didn't think I looked good enough to compete with girls their age. They assured me I did and kept urging me to at least try it. They told me to stop by in the middle of the afternoon when it wasn't busy and to bring an outfit to wear in case I was put onstage. It made me nervous just thinking about walking into a place like that. I'd never been in a strip club and what would everyone think? Why would a girl be going there?

Well, I *had* to go -- I mean I had to see what the whole thing was about. I could just sit there and watch. I could leave after two minutes if I wanted to. I did want to see what the girls actually did. How did they dance around and seductively take off their clothes? I wanted to learn how to do that.

I threw one of Darlene's outfits in a bag even though I was sure I wouldn't really get up there and dance. I would have to *study* how to do it first and then go home and practice.

I got as far as the parking lot, but then I started having second thoughts. That sick feeling was in my stomach -- the feeling I used to get when I was in high school and the teacher would surprise us with a test and I knew I wasn't ready for it and would definitely flunk it. Impending disaster. I sat in the car for a few minutes. I watched some of the men going in and out. Would these men want to look at me, I mean as a group? And they will have been drinking, which meant they'd be uninhibited. If they were turned off by my age, they wouldn't be polite about it. They'd just holler out something horribly rude. I'd be humiliated and lose all the confidence I'd built up from playing Darlene.

I made up my mind that I'd just go in, watch for ten minutes, and leave. There. It was decided. "Fifteen minutes from now, it will all be over, and I'll feel so proud of myself."

When I walked in, there was this guy at the door who looked like a walrus. He was a fat slob and even had those walrussy whiskers. He sort of blocked the entrance and just stared at me as if to say, "What the hell do you want?" I was hoping I could just slip in unnoticed, but it was clear that the walrus expected me to say something.

"A couple of my friends work here. They said it would be okay if I came in." He still said nothing but stepped aside. I looked around for the best place to hide, saw an empty booth, and slid into it. It was about 2:30, and although it was a big room, there weren't many people there. There were lots of empty tables out on the floor and a few empty booths around the perimeter of the room. A girl came over, said her name was Bambi, and asked if I'd like something to drink. I told her I had just stopped by to see Katie and Samantha and would only be there for a couple of minutes. She said she'd tell them I was there and added that soft drinks were free for the ladies, so I asked for a diet Coke.

Katie showed up right away and said, "You're just in time. Samantha's up next." Katie sat with me and we watched her. Wow. Of course I'd seen her in the outfits she wore at the dungeon, and I'd seen her nude there, but this was a different kind of theater. She was up on a stage, the lighting was very dramatic, and there was *music*. She was moving to the music and I, being a dancer, was completely swept away by the creativity of her performance. She chose not only her costume and music, but also the lighting. She picked the colors of all of those bulbs hanging over the stage and on the floor around the front edge of it. She created the exact mood she wanted.

Katie explained that each girl did a three-song set, and by the end of the third song she had to lose her bra. She didn't have to take off the g-string because this was only a topless club, not a nude one. During Samantha's set, some of the men who had been standing a distance from the stage walked toward it and sat at the rail. They each took out at least one bill and laid it over the bar there. After the third song ended, she went around the edge of the stage and picked up all of the money. Then she retrieved the parts of her costume that she'd taken off and thrown to the sides of the stage. She added the bills to the money that was already in a large, old-fashioned glass that she'd brought out onstage with her and placed in plain view. Backstage, she got dressed (In a different outfit), came out, and joined Katie and me.

I told her I thought she was fantastic and that I wanted to learn to do the same thing. "Learn? There's nothing to learn. Just pick an attitude. And I'll tell you what lighting to use." Then she said, "I'll ask Ralph if he'll put you up." I grabbed her arm.

"Oh wait! I'm not ready. I want to see what the rest of the girls do and then go home and practice. I have to figure this all out ahead of time." Samantha thought that was very funny.

"Oh, God, Darlene. You're such a *teacher*. Did you bring an outfit?" I told her I did, but I didn't have any music. (I was looking for an excuse to postpone this). She said, "The

DJ has an inventory. You probably want something soft and romantic." Exactly. Samantha knew Darlene. She had worked with me long enough at the dungeon. She was gone a couple of minutes during which time Katie continued the pep talk. Samantha came back and triumphantly announced that everything was set. She'd spoken to Ralph and the DJ, and chosen the lighting and music. "Let's go back and get you dressed. You're up after the next girl." The feeling of terror returned.

The little voice in my head was talking to me. "Oh God. What have I gotten myself into? This is either going to be wonderful or dreadful." I wanted it to be over. I wanted to be home and safe and to be able to think back on it, but I didn't want to have to go through it. I started getting dressed, but I hesitated when I picked up the garter belt. I said to Samantha in a worried tone, "Maybe I shouldn't wear the stockings. The other girls are all bare-legged." She knew better.

"Wear them. That's who Darlene is."

"But most of those guys out there are cowboy types and bikers. They won't like me. They'll walk away from the stage."

"Trust me. You'll get enough."

The current dancer had just finished and stepped into the dressing area carrying her bra and old-fashioned glass. I heard the DJ announce that a new girl was being put in the rotation and said my name. Oh God. I was nauseated again.

The introduction to some soft music was beginning to play. Samantha held the curtain back, gave me a little shove, and said, "Now just be Darlene."

I soon recognized the melody. It was "Just My Imagination" by the Temptations. I had always liked that song and let myself fall into it. I drifted. I floated. I was in my own little world. By the end of it, I hadn't taken off anything, and I figured that during the second song I'd take off the lacy negligee that covered my bra, g-string, and Darlene's signature garter belt.

Then the lighting changed. That Samantha had thought of everything. The next song was "Hold On My Heart" by Phil Collins. Another perfect choice. And even though I could barely walk in such high heels, I had to. I had to move gracefully and look good doing it. So I got lost in Phil, moved the straps of the slip over my shoulders and let it fall to the floor. I stepped out of it with one foot and used the other to kick it to the side of the stage.

Song three. The lighting changed again. Another Phil Collins song, "Do You Remember?" One of my absolute favorites. How *did* she know? I finally started to relax a little, enough to take a peek at what was happening *out there*, beyond the footlights. There were only a couple of vacant seats at the rail, about the same as during Samantha's set. Thank you God. They like me after all. *That many men* were sitting at the rail. I felt warm. And desired. And...yes...*powerful.* I was seven years old all over again. I thought, "I know why they're here. They want to see what's behind the bra." *And* I wanted them to see what was behind the bra. And I wanted to see their faces at that instant. I stepped closer to them, as close as I legally could. Samantha had told me I couldn't really dance to the rail. I had to stay behind a tape mark a couple of feet in front of it. I made eye contact with a few of them as I got closer and the song was coming to its end. I saw that mesmerized look in their eyes, the look I craved. I unhooked the bra and turned around revealing my bare back. I was still holding the bra in place with one hand. I turned again and faced the men. As the song ended, I lifted my hand. I felt like a goddess.

The music had ended, and the spell had been broken. Back to reality. I picked up the bra and started walking to where my slip lay when I heard Samantha call out from the side of the stage, "Darlene! Get the money!" I started at one end and went bill by bill sometimes looking at the men who were still sitting there. A few pointed to various locations in the room and indicated that they wanted to talk to me. Because of the lights, I couldn't see them clearly enough to be able to recognize them again, and I told Samantha. I mean they had given me money, and I didn't want to be rude and ignore them. She wasn't the least bit concerned and said, "Don't go looking for any of them. They'll find you."

At that point, I didn't really want to be found. I just wanted to put my street clothes on again and go home. I only had the one outfit with me, and I wasn't on the schedule anyhow. So, I put on my baggy jeans and loose-fitting surgeon's top (very sexy) and followed Samantha back out on the floor. I was planning to leave immediately, but there were a few interruptions. A man came over, said "Enjoyed the show," and pressed a business card into my palm. Another one actually said, "Here's my card. I'd really like to take you to dinner sometime."

I gave Samantha a questioning look as if to say, "Is this all right? Can they do this?"

She shrugged her shoulders and said, "Oh, you'll get a collection...Now let's go see Ralph." Ralph, remember, was the guy at the door who, it turned out, made the schedule.

The walrus finally spoke. It gave me no feedback on my performance and merely grunted, "When can you work?"

I told him Monday through Thursday, during the day. I was still teaching school those four nights, and the other three evenings I was at the dungeon.

Darlene had become a *very* busy girl.

In the Bathroom

When this client came in there were no rooms available. We had five, but there were already sessions going on. It turned out that this was perfect for this client because he wanted his session to take place in the bathroom.

He looked like an ordinary college kid and was wearing jeans, a T-shirt, and Nikes. I was his older sister and I had seen him jacking off one day while wearing my underwear (one of my bras and a pair of my panties). So one day I decided to really humiliate him. I shoved him into the bathroom, stepped inside, and locked the door behind us. *Also,* I made him put on my bra and panties. (Actually, the client had brought a bra and panties with him for this purpose).

Then I told him to stand in front of the toilet and start playing with himself. I said I would not allow him to leave the bathroom until he had successfully come into the toilet. I also told him that if he missed the toilet he would have to clean up the mess he made. While he was doing this, I further degraded him by telling him what a loser he was and how he would never have a girlfriend. He would spend the rest of his life masturbating while wearing women's underwear. Throughout all of this he complained, whined, and begged to be let out of the bathroom. I stood right in front of the door and there was nothing he could do.

Then I started telling him that he had better hurry up because our parents were going to be coming home soon and, of course, he wouldn't want them to see what was going on now would he? "Come on now. Hurry up! Show me what a loser you really are, you worthless sissy... Mom and dad will be home any minute. Do you want them to find out what a lousy excuse for a son you are? You'll never have a girlfriend or a wife or children. You're a disgrace to this family." I went on and on.

Eventually he came, and most of his cum did *not* land in the toilet, and, yes, I *did* make him stay there. There were towels and rubbing alcohol in the bathroom, and I made him get down on his hands and knees and clean up his pitiful mess. Then he took off "my" bra and panties and put them back in the bag he had brought with him.

We made eye contact, and it was understood that we now had a secret that would never be shared with anyone.

*The picture quality is not so great, but I swear
it's me enjoying my time on stage during high school.*

Senior portrait.

In the classroom.

On an acting job. Look how sweet and innocent I look!

A casual shot.

Darlene at work.

*This was taken not long before I "became Darlene" during a time
I was active in church. The man in the photo is a very
well-known religious leader in Los Angeles. I'm
sure he would have started praying right then and
there if he had known of Darlene's upcoming "birth."
-Photo courtesy of the author's private collection*

In the Morgue

I thought of this client as the coroner. I never knew his name. His was a rather elaborate session and he sent me instructions ahead of time. Four ladies were needed for at least two hours. Our dungeon was to be a "morgue." Three of the ladies were deceased, and I was the "angel of death." Prior to the start of the session, I was to prepare the room by lighting an abundance of white candles all over the room. On a table, I was to place one red candle and a small gold-colored pitcher. The three ladies were to lie on their backs on the floor, and I was to drape two of them with towels covering their entire bodies. All of the ladies were nude, including myself. There was to be no conversation. The action had been described in the instructions, and I had explained the entire scenario to the ladies. We were about to act out a death ritual. The session began when the client entered the room.

He walked to where I was sitting and stood next to me. I rose and walked to where one of the covered ladies lay. I removed the towel from her body, sank to my knees, and sat on my feet. Then I leaned over and kissed her forehead, which brought her back to life. She rose and followed me to where the uncovered lady lay, the lady who was being honored. We knelt beside her. We crossed ourselves, bowed our heads, and prayed. I then stood and went to the table to get the pitcher, which contained a special oil. I poured the oil over the breasts of the still deceased lady. The newly risen lady then massaged the oil into the dead lady's breasts until it was completely absorbed. Then both of us rose and I escorted her back to where she had been lying. She returned to her starting position, lying on her back. I knelt beside her and kissed her on her forehead. She was once again dead. I covered her body with the towel.

I then walked to the second covered lady and went through the same actions to raise her from the dead. She followed me to the side of the honored one. We knelt, crossed ourselves, bowed our heads, and prayed. I then stood and went to the table to get the red candle. I handed it to the newly risen lady, who proceeded to dribble the candle wax on the torso of the honored lady. She began at the base of her throat and moved down to her pubic bone. Then she went sideways, from one nipple to the other, thus creating a cross. She handed the candle back to me, and I returned it to the table. I then walked back to lady number two and escorted her back to her original location. She lay on her back, and I knelt and kissed her forehead. She was again among the dead. I covered her body with the towel.

At this point the client's instructions told me to return to my chair and simply witness what was to occur. The client, who had been dressed the whole time, walked to the honored lady. He stood over her breasts, straddling her body, facing her head. He was wearing a black long-sleeved shirt, black pants, and black shoes. He unzipped his pants, reached in, and pulled out his penis. He began stroking himself. After a few minutes, he came all over the lady's breasts. Then he stood there for several minutes more, just staring at her. Finally, he zipped up his pants and left the room. That was the end of the session.

This whole thing took about two hours. Usually the desk person buzzes on the intercom when the time is up, but this client did not want that to be done. He wanted no interruptions, no noise.

So there I was with the three other ladies in the dungeon. We all knew that when the client left the room, the session was over. They simply got up and joined me in cleaning up. We gathered the towels we had used and sprayed rubbing alcohol on the table and chair. The *honored* one was kind of a mess, of course. She had had oil rubbed into her breasts, candle wax poured on her, and semen squirted on her. She went to the bathroom and took a shower.

The client had spoken to none of us. He had only communicated with me, ahead of time, in writing. Our tips were left for us at the desk, in sealed envelopes.

Just another afternoon of play.

Daily Life

During this eighteen year period, I worked at a few dungeons, danced in numerous strip clubs, and taught at a handful of different school sites. All of my teaching was done for the same school district, and most of it took place at the same school. This particular school was located in the same neighborhood as the dungeon where I spent most of my years as Darlene. That's right. The school where I spent Monday through Thursday teaching high school subjects was in the same zip code as the bondage parlor where Darlene spent Friday through Sunday tying up men's testicles with rope. My students not only attended the school in the neighborhood, they also *lived* there. I saw my students' addresses on their registration forms and thought, "Oh, Miguel lives a block away from the dungeon." Some lived just down the street and may have even driven, bicycled, or even walked right past it on their way to class -- Ms. ______'s class, not Darlene's class.

Oh, wait. Hold on. Let me check. What day is it? Occasionally, I forgot where I was going and drove to the dungeon instead of the school or vice versa. And sometimes I forgot who I was supposed to be when I got there. Many times over the years someone at school asked my name and I said, "Dar---, uh Ms. ______." And *then*, just for the fun of it, I said things at school that made sense coming out of Darlene's mouth, but not Ms. ______'s. For example, when a student wouldn't stop talking, I'd say, "Now Julio, if you're talking continues, I'll have to go out and get my black leather riding crop from the trunk of my car." I knew no one believed I really had one there -- along with a whip, handcuffs, and a bag of gadgets used for cock and ball torture.

Since I was working in the same neighborhood seven days a week, I ran other errands there, too. I'd leave the dungeon and stop at the local grocery store on my way home. And who did I see at the store? My students of course. Some shopped there, and some worked there. One worked in the produce department, one in the *panaderia* (bakery), and two were baggers. Other employees knew who I was -- a teacher at the local school. Even the manager told me his wife attended my school to learn English when she first came here from Mexico. So here I was, bumping into my own students at the businesses in the area. Didn't it also make sense that I would run into *clients* at these places? Of course, it made sense, but it never happened. Amazing.

What's even more amazing is that none of my students ever came into the dungeon. Some students were high school kids, but the adults could have walked right in. Maybe they didn't know the place was there. After all, it was a nondescript building with nothing written on it, not even the address. Or maybe since they were still trying to earn high school diplomas, they weren't interested in spending a lot of money to be tied up and tortured. But there was one thing I was sure would happen eventually. Someday a student was bound to show up delivering food. At the dungeon, there were three shifts with about six ladies on each one, and the shifts overlapped. So there were half a dozen to a dozen of us just hanging around for several hours waiting for clients to come in. It was a comfortable place to "live" with many creature comforts. We could watch TV, read, talk on the phone, play on the computers, and even sleep. I sat in the lounge and corrected school work. "What did you bring today, Darlene? World history or algebra?"

There was a kitchen area equipped with a refrigerator, microwave, and coffee pot, but we didn't take lunch breaks. We never left the building during our shifts, so we had to have food delivered, and we did -- many times a day. Pizza, Thai, Mexican. A guy would come in the front door, and the man at the desk would holler, "Fooooood." Then the lady who had ordered it would part the curtain concealing the lounge and step into the lobby to pay him. The delivery person rarely spoke English, which meant he could also have been an English as a Second Language student at the neighborhood adult school. I was even looking forward to the day when "Juan" would show up with tacos, and the lady paying him would be his teacher, Ms. ______, wearing a black lace bustier, her 36D breasts popping out the top. I wondered if "Juan" would have the nerve to show up at school the next day. I really got a kick out of tempting fate, and it went on -- year after year. The school, the dungeon, the dungeon, the school. Same neighborhood, same person -- me. But no one recognized me. And the event that I was sure would happen never did. "Juan" never came in the dungeon, no one ever put two and two together, and the school district remained oblivious.

Of course, now that I'm writing about it, the school district will finally know. Oh. Wait a minute. That won't happen either. It's common knowledge that no one in the administration building in *this* school district knows how to read.

John Byrd

John Byrd was from Australia. He was huge. He was about six foot five and built like a football player. On top of that he was overweight. He wanted to be restrained and tickled. It's funny he chose the smallest lady there to tie him up.

So here's what we did: He took off all his clothes. I had him lie down on the bondage table on his stomach. I put furry wrist cuffs on each wrist and attached is arms to the rings on the table. I did the same thing to his ankles so that when I was finished, he looked like a big X on the table. He wanted me to be nude also. I started with his head. I began caressing him, lightly touching him, his head, his neck, his shoulders his arms his fingers, down his back his rear end, the backs of his thighs, his calves and his feet. He especially wanted his feet tickled.

He twitched when I tickled them, but he couldn't move much because, remember, his feet were tied to the table.

After about half an hour of this, I turned him over so he was lying on his back and fastened his wrists and ankles to the table again. Then I started with his face, his forehead, cheeks and lips. When I was at his lips, he tried to lick and even suck on my fingers. I continued down his body, barely touching his chest, his nipples, and his stomach. I skipped his private parts and went to his thighs and, eventually, his feet again. I spent more time on his feet than anything else. All the time I was doing this, he was talking to me about Australia. He had a ranch there, and he told me about all of the animals and his daily life there, but when I got to his feet he stopped talking. It seemed he didn't want any distractions when it came to his feet.

Toward the end of the session, I released one of his hands and handed him the bottle of oil so that he could play with himself. While he did that, he wanted me to keep tickling his feet. He liked the way I touched him - my light touch. He said I had magic fingers.

He came back to see me several times over a period of about three years.

The Credit Card Problem

This session was another role play. I was the wife of the client and apparently I was a shopaholic. In the past I had charged too much on my credit cards and gone over the limit. My husband had told me that I had a problem controlling my impulses.

"Children have trouble controlling their impulses. I love you, but if you continue to behave like a child I'll have to treat you like a child."

I had ignored him. After all, I *always* got what I wanted.

Our session began with my husband already inside the room and with me outside in the hall. Having just come from shopping, I breezed into the room carrying several bags and said, "Oh hi, honey, I'm home. How's everything?" I was delighted that my husband had finished work early and was there waiting for me. I wanted to model my new outfits for him, but the expression on his face made me nervous. He was glaring at me, which meant that he was unhappy.

"I'm sorry, sweetie, but I warned you." I gave him my best wide-eyed, innocent, what-in-the-world-are-you-talking-about look. "You just couldn't control yourself, could you? You've gone over the limit again and we've been charged another fee."

I pretended to take him seriously, but he didn't buy it.

"You've acted like a child, and now, as I told you, I'm going to have to treat you like a child."

"Oh, I understand. No ice cream for me tonight, huh?" I was *really* hoping he'd laugh, but no such luck. He took me by the hand and led me to a chair. He sat. I expected him to sit me on his lap so that we could have a serious daddy/daughter talk. Was I in for a surprise. He pulled me over his lap, lifted my skirt, pulled down my panties, and gave me a hefty swat. I shrieked. I hadn't been spanked since I was a small child so I was appalled. And pissed. I yelled, "What do you think you're doing?" and tried to wiggle off his lap, but he was much stronger than I was and had no trouble holding me down. He continued spanking me, so I kept up my hollering.

"What's wrong with you? You can't do this! You can't hit me like that! You can't spank me as if I were a child! I'm your wife!" I was making some major noise, but I knew no one was going to come to my rescue. The other ladies wouldn't come charging through the door to save me unless I uttered the "code words" which meant that I *really* needed help. Until those magic words were heard, the guy at the front desk would ignore me, although he would giggle some. He thought it was kind of humorous that I took my acting so seriously.

Even though I was throwing a huge tantrum, my husband was surprisingly calm. He kept on whacking me while speaking in a perfunctory manner. "You behaved like a child, so I have no choice but to punish you like a child -- and there's nothing you can do about it."

I was outraged. I shouted, "Stop! You're *hurting* me! I'm getting very sore."

He chuckled and replied, "That's the idea. I want you to get sore and stay sore for a long time so that you'll remember this and finally learn your lesson."

I then went into crying mode and whined, "*Pleeease!* You've spanked me enough. I've learned my lesson. I promise I won't do it again."

This tactic didn't work.

He shook his head and said, "Oh, no. You're not getting out of this that easily. I can tell you haven't learned anything yet. Your cheeks aren't nearly as red as I want them to be." And with that, he started to spank me even harder. This went on for a few more minutes. Then he stopped. I thought he was finished, but it turned out that he only stopped to rest his hand and have a little conversation. He continued speaking in that annoying, mechanical tone. "All right now. Let's review what happened today. What did you do?"

I was still bawling but managed to respond, "I w-went sh-shopping."

"And what did you buy?"

I confessed everything (with the hope of enticing him). "A couple of *low-cut* blouses, a very *short* skirt, a pair of shoes with *spiked* heels, a new purse, and several pairs of *black* stockings."

He was unaffected. He simply stated, "You're taking all of it back."

I still wasn't about to give up and argued back. "Oh no! The blouses are exactly what I've been looking for and the shoes and purse match perfectly. I don't want to take them back!"

"That's too bad, little lady. Everything is going back, *and* you no longer have credit card privileges." I started to open my mouth again, but he interrupted me. "See, I told you you haven't been taught well enough. You need to be spanked more. Ten more swats and I want to hear you count."

"Only ten more. I can live through this," I thought to myself. I didn't want to squabble any longer.

He started in. The first smack. I recited, "One." The next one. "Two." This man was using his open hand and putting a lot of energy into it. I just hoped that his hand was getting as sore as my rear end was. Ten finally came. "Ten." So we were done. Were we done? He didn't move. He didn't let me up right away. (psychological torture)

"Now you can get up." He took my hand and walked me over to the wall where there was a mirror. He made me turn around and lift up my skirt. "See, how red your little ass is? I bet it hurts doesn't it? I want you to remember how sore it is, and if you do this again your punishment will be much worse. Now take all your packages outside and put everything in the car because we're going back to the mall together and return everything right now."

I was done acting like a brat. I timidly gathered the bags I'd brought in and quietly left the room. I set the bags just outside the door and just waited there. There were a couple of ladies sitting in the lounge at the other end of the hall, and I knew they could see me, but I didn't make eye contact with them. I was still in character. If this client wanted me to be the disobedient, little-girl wife all the way until he left the building, I was going to do it. It was *his* fantasy, and I wanted to be the best at giving it to him.

A few minutes later my husband came out of the room. He paused, looked down at me, and gave me a stern look as if to say, "Remember this you bad little girl you." I reacted to this "scolding" by lowering my head and staring at the floor. Having done his parental duty, he walked on down the hall to the front desk.

The Rubber Band Man

During the interview, this client told me he wanted to be castrated. He hadn't been able to *impress* (he wanted me to use that word) me and that was to be his punishment. He had brought his own rubber band for me to use. That was enough for me to go on, so off we went to a dungeon that looked like something left over from the Spanish Inquisition -- a black bondage table, a black suspension bar hanging from the ceiling, and a black cross which was used for crucifixion fantasies. On the walls hung ropes of various lengths, whips, and chains. This guy was about six feet tall and had a husky build, like a football player. He had some muscles all right, but there was definitely a layer of fat on top. Good. Something for me to criticize. He said his name was Karl.

We entered the room, I pushed the button on the intercom, and a voice said, "Thank you."

I spoke in my most authoritative voice. "You know you've disappointed me, don't you Karl? And you know what's about to happen."

"Yes, mistress." He looked at the floor. He knew better than to try to make eye contact. And his voice had become very soft and weak. He knew he deserved his punishment.

"Take off your clothes and stand under the suspension bar."

"Yes, mistress." He folded his clothes neatly and left them on the bondage table along with a little bag.

The suspension bar was a block of wood about four inches by four inches, and about five feet long. Although it was above his head at the moment, in order for me to tie him to it, I had to lower it to where I could reach it. Even with my spike heels, I was only five feet four. It was attached to a heavy chain and could be cranked up or down. As I lowered it, the sound of the links banging against each other was quite loud, setting a chilling mood. Torture was about to take place.

Using rope, I tied each wrist to a metal loop at each end of the bar. I then tied his ankles to the posts at each side of the bar. He wasn't going anywhere. I cranked the bar up so that his arms were spread above his head, and now he looked like a big "X." I laid towels on the floor in what I thought was the right spot for later. Then I pulled up a chair a few feet in front of him. I sat down and crossed my legs. There I was, looking all sweet and sexy in one of Darlene's lacy negligees, but holding a black leather riding crop.

"Look at you now, Karl. You really screwed up. I had such high hopes for you, but now you've left me no choice."

"You're right, mistress."

"Men who don't know how to use their cocks lose their privileges."

"I know, mistress."

"There's nothing you want to say in your own defense?"

"No, mistress."

"Then, we'll begin."

I assumed that the rubber band he'd brought was in the bag on the bondage table, so I walked over, picked up the bag, and dangled it in front of him in a threatening manner as I walked back to my chair. When I looked inside, what I saw wasn't at all what I was expecting. I knew rubber bands came in different widths and thicknesses, but this one was round, like a little inner tube. And it was thick, about 1/3" in diameter. *And*, the hole in the middle wasn't very big. How did he expect me to get even one testicle through it, let alone two? I took the little tube thing out and held it in front of his face.

"Look at this, Karl. This is going to be very painful, but you know you deserve it."

"Yes, mistress."

I reached down, located one of his balls, and positioned it against the opening of the band. Of course, the hole wasn't big enough, but I figured if I stretched the band while shoving the ball, I could get it to pop through. It was *not* easy. Karl should have chosen a lady who looked as if she'd been working out with heavy weights. It took a few tries, but I finally met with success. One down, one to go.

I used the same procedure with the other ball, and eventually I was able to push it through. I looked up at Karl's face to see if I could detect any pain, but there was none. I decided he was a bite-the-bullet type. But, really. It *had* to hurt like hell. This little tube was at the base of his balls, a lot of tissue was squeezed inside it, and his balls were bulging. The skin around them was stretched so tightly, it looked like something was going to pop. I was nervous. I sat on my chair in front of him and struck a sexy pose.

"Well, Karl. How do you like your punishment now?"

"It's what I deserve mistress. I let you down. I wasn't able to impress you."

"You know the circulation is being cut off. The pain is going to get worse, and then your testicles will drop off."

"I deserve to lose them mistress."

Karl must have liked whatever pain he was in because he had an erection. I tapped his cock with my crop, and was it ever hard.

"So, Karl, let's review. What got you here in the first place? What did you do?"

"Well, mistress, I was playing with my cock without permission, and I got caught."

"And what is the rule about that, Karl?"

"The rule is that I'm only allowed to do that in front of you and with your permission."

"So why did you disobey?"

"Because I'd been thinking about you a lot and couldn't stand it any longer. I couldn't wait to see you. I thought I could get away with masturbating just once."

"Arrogance, Karl. Admit it. You were being arrogant."

"Yes, mistress, I was."

"You've also been lazy lately, Karl. Look at you. Your body used to be nicely toned, and now your muscles don't show at all. There's a layer of disgusting fat over them. What do you have to say about that?"

"I know you're right, mistress. I haven't been working out as much as I used to."

"Discipline, Karl. A lack of discipline."

"Yes, mistress. I'm guilty of that too."

"So what do you think about where you are now?"

"I'm where I should be, mistress. I deserve to be neutered like an animal."

"At least you're being humble. I like that. I also like your apologetic tone." I acted as if I were thinking things over. "How's the pain now Karl?"

"It's getting worse, mistress. A lot worse."

"Poor Karl. You know you do have a couple of redeeming qualities after all, and this is the first time you broke the rule. I'm considering giving you another chance."

"I don't deserve it, mistress."

"I like your attitude Karl, and for some reason I'm feeling very charitable today. I'll give you one more opportunity to impress me, and if you can, I won't castrate you today. What do you think, Karl? Do you think you'd be able to impress me now?"

"Oh yes, mistress. Please, if you would allow me to try one more time, I promise I would never break the rule again."

"Very good, Karl. I believe you have learned your lesson. I'll remove the band now."

I got up from my chair and stepped toward him with the intention of pulling the band off.

"Excuse me, mistress. It won't come off that way. You have to cut it off. I brought something. It's in the bag."

I looked in, expecting to find scissors, but instead found a plastic container. When I opened it, I was horrified. It was a razor blade. Was he kidding? A *razor blade*? He wanted me to *slice* through the band with a blade that sharp? That was dangerous. If I pushed too hard, I could end up really cutting into his testicles, and if I didn't aim in the right direction, I could cut into my own fingers. I did *not* want to try this at all. And for him to even trust me to do this, was he *crazy*?

"Are you sure about this, Karl?"

"Yes, mistress. I trust you."

I wanted to chuckle at what I thought was a ridiculous comment, but then it occurred to me that perhaps the danger added to his excitement. After all, it was his razor blade.

I don't know what happened in my head, but my fear went away and was replaced by the desire to do the dangerous thing. I decided to go for it.

I held the razor blade against the rubber and began to press gently. Since those blades are so sharp, I thought slight pressure would be enough. The blade would cut right through, and this would be over. But no. I would have to press harder. I did and felt the blade making progress, but now there was another problem. How would I know when I was almost through to the other side? The rubber might snap off, I'd still be pressing, and I'd cut into his flesh. All I could do was tell myself to *pay attention*.

It certainly wasn't due to my skill since I'd never done this before, so it must have been just luck. The blade went through the band, I felt it give way, and I stopped pressing. I let the little tube drop to the floor, and I stepped back. I set the razor blade down and once again picked up my riding crop. I wasn't finished with Karl yet. I squirted his still erect cock with oil, untied one of his wrists, and sat down to watch the show.

"All right, Karl. Now's your chance. *Impress* me."

"Thank you, mistress. I will. I'll show you what I can do. I'll impress you."

"Yes, Karl. *Impress* me. I know you want to. Impress me, Karl. That's right. *Impress me. Impress...*"

Wow. I *was* impressed. His cum spurted out at least a foot before dropping to the floor. Fortunately, it landed on one of the aforementioned towels.

"Very, very good, Karl."

He just laughed. It was over. The spell was broken and he wasn't Karl anymore. I untied his other wrist and his ankles. He got dressed. No conversation. He took a folded-up bill from his pocket and gave it to me. I didn't look at it -- that would have been rude. I assumed it was twenty dollars. That's typical for a 30 minute session. I walked with him to the front desk. He kissed me on the cheek.

I never saw him again.

Oh, the face on the bill didn't turn out to be Jackson's. It was Grant's.

A Saturday Treat

Mistress Lydia had her own private dungeon at the Castle. Private. It was the only room that was locked. Only she and the owner had the key. She also had a personal slave, Dave (think Ed Asner at thirty-five). During the week he was an ordinary businessman, but on weekends he was at her beck and call. It was common knowledge that he cleaned her house, ran errands, and even washed her car. The first Saturday of the month was his day to serve at the Castle. That meant he had to spend the day doing whatever any of the ladies asked him to do such as fetching coffee, giving a foot massage, or cleaning the bathroom. While awaiting orders, his assigned place was in the lounge on the floor. He was never allowed to sit on furniture. He crawled around on all fours, like a dog, and wore only a black leather dog collar. That's right. He was nude. Since he spent most of his time in the lounge, he was visible to all of the clients even if they just walked through the lounge on their way to a room. Many clients, though, spent a least a few minutes sitting in the lounge waiting for one of the ladies, watching TV, or just chatting. Dave was not allowed to talk to them. In fact, he wasn't allowed to talk to anyone. When one of the ladies gave him a command, he was only permitted to say, "Yes, mistress."

This particular Saturday was Mistress Lydia's birthday. Dave had arrived with a dozen long-stemmed red roses, which were prominently displayed on the coffee table in the lounge. Little did Dave know that he would be giving his mistress another present later in the evening. You need to understand that Mistress Lydia loved owning things. She had her own dungeon, her own equipment, and her own slave. The dungeon had her name on the door, and her equipment had her initials on it. But here was her slave, Dave, without so much as a name tag. That was to change tonight.

By the time the mistress arrived at 6 P.M., her slave had been there for hours dutifully serving. She asked the rest of us to rate his work so far that day. We gave him a thumbs up. We liked Dave, and he loved being ordered around. Then the mistress announced that she had a special treat for us that evening involving Dave. It would take place in her dungeon at nine, and all were invited. I looked forward to this event. I had gotten to observe a couple of Mistress Lydia's sessions in the past, and they had been very educational. She had some personal equipment that the rest of us weren't allowed to use. I knew I'd learn something interesting.

Nine o'clock arrived and Mistress Lydia entered the lounge holding a leash, which she attached to Dave's collar. She was radiant, as usual. The mistress was six feet tall in her stocking feet and had long, fluffy blonde hair half way down her back. She wore a black leather bustier, a black thong, mesh stockings, and black, thigh-high leather boots with spike heels that now made her six foot five. Wow.

"Follow me, everyone. The show is about to begin."

She gave her slave's collar a yank, and he eagerly crawled after her all the way down the long hall to her dungeon. Poor Dave.

Several other ladies and I followed and were told to stand around the bondage table. Dave was ordered to crawl on top and lie on his stomach. The mistress used rope to tie his wrists and ankles to the rings at each of the four corners. She then unzipped a black leather case and took out a butane lighter and a knife. A few of us gasped. That knife looked evil. She sat on the table near Dave's rear end, turned on the flame, and held the blade in it. She began to explain.

"Ladies, I believe it's very important to label one's property. As many of you know, Dave has been mine for several years, and I thought it was high time I put my mark on him. So I'm going to brand him tonight with my initials. He'll never serve another mistress."

There was a stunned silence. I, for one, had second thoughts about being there. I wasn't sure I wanted to witness this after all. Would there be blood? Would it spray all over the place? Would I pass out? I decided to stay because I thought even if all of the above happened, it wouldn't be the end of the world. Besides, I might never get another chance to see such a bizarre demonstration.

Mistress Lydia continued with her narration of the process. "You see, ladies, the heat from the fire disinfects the knife. I wouldn't want my slave to get sick from harmful bacteria." The tone of her voice amused me. She spoke as casually as someone giving a cooking demonstration on a morning talk show. "Fiona, would you assist me by taking a cotton ball, saturating it with rubbing alcohol, and wiping this area of my slave's ass?" The mistress used the knife to point to Dave's right cheek. "Very good, Fiona. We're ready. I'm going to carve a capital M and L diagonally. Here we go." The whole time the mistress was talking to us, Dave did nothing. I guess he knew about this ahead of time and was mentally prepared. So she began. She turned off the flame, set the lighter down, and pressed the knife into the flesh. There was a sizzling sound as if someone were cooking bacon. But this didn't smell at all like bacon -- or pork, or beef, or chicken, or any- thing I'd ever smelled. It was some kind of meat, but this was a foul odor, certainly not appetizing. The mistress held the knife in position for only a few seconds. When she lifted it, I could see blood, but it didn't run. It coagulated almost imme-diately. Very tidy I thought. And what about Dave? His response was almost imperceptible. His eyes closed tightly and his hamstring muscles tightened, but he made no noise. What a good little slave. Mistress Lydia turned on the lighter again and held the knife in it. "We have to make sure the blade is hot enough each time."

I continued to watch Dave. I tried to put myself in his place and imagine what he was thinking. Was he feeling pain? The mistress had five more strokes to go. Was he wishing the ordeal were over or was he really a masochist and enjoying the sting of the blade? I would never know. Five more times, the mistress pressed the knife into his skin. We heard the sizzle and smelled that smell -- sickening. Dave did start to sweat, but to be truthful, I was hoping for more. I wanted to see him squirm -- I mean really writhe in agony. This was supposed to be torture. I wanted to see some drama. The second stroke of the "L" and the mistress was finished. "Fiona, would you please squirt Dave's ass with the rubbing alcohol? Thank you, ladies. Enjoy the rest of the evening."

Mistress Lydia. What a gal.

Kenny

Here's a fun client. Kenny was about six foot four. He was a very well-built guy, and was really a very good looking man or would have been. You see, I never saw Kenny dressed as a man. He arrived dressed in drag. He wore a dress, stockings, pumps, a wig, ear rings, and was in full make-up.

Our session began like this: He lay on his back on the floor in our room. I proceeded to wrap him up in clear plastic wrap from head to toe like a mummy. Immediately after wrapping his head, I would poke holes near his nose and mouth so that he could breathe. I also made openings for his eyes. So there he was, all wrapped up, staring up at the ceiling. My job was to videotape him as he squirmed around on the floor. He had brought his own video camera and shown me how to operate it during the interview. He began wiggling around like a worm. He would scrunch up his body and then extend it the way caterpillars do. That way he was able to make some progress moving around the floor. He even made his way to the door of the dungeon, at which time I was to open the door and allow him to crawl outside into the hall. So, there was this six foot four inch man, dressed as a woman and wrapped in plastic, crawling around on the floor in the hallway. No more privacy in the dungeon. He was *in the hall*, which meant that other people in the Castle could see him -- not only the ladies but also the other clients.

What was amazing, was that the clients didn't pay much attention to him. They looked over and saw him, but then they immediately ignored him as if they had seen such goings on every day. It seemed to be no big deal that I was videotaping the whole thing. He wanted close ups of his face as well as the rest of his body. He also wanted the whole scene from a distance. He wanted me to go way down to the other end of the long hall and videotape him squirming his way down it. Eventually, he slithered his way back into the dungeon. We only had a few minutes left, so I took a pair of scissors and cut an opening for one of his hands and part of his arm. I also cut an opening between his legs. He reached under his dress and somehow pulled it up. Then he pulled his panties aside.

After that, I squirted some oil you-know-where and he proceeded to jack off. Per his instructions, I taped the whole thing. His aim was very good. He didn't make any mess on the floor.   His semen shot up in the air and landed on his upper body.

After I unwrapped him, he wadded up all the plastic with his semen on it and disposed of it for me in a very tidy way. After all, he was dressed as a lady, and he left dressed that way. He didn't bring any other clothes to change into. He had been coming to the Castle for some time, and the slave behind the desk knew him well. Several of the ladies who had been there a while knew him well also. They didn't even look up when he walked through the lounge and casually said, "Oh, hi Ken."

That was the end of my session with him, but he did come in a couple of other times when I was there and did sessions with other ladies. One time he came in, dressed in drag of course, and she wrapped him up just as I had. Then a couple of slaves (men) who were hanging around carried him to the back of a pickup truck, where he was placed on his back. After that, the lady doing the session would drive around town with him lying there. Since there are some vehicles that are raised high off the ground, passengers could see into the back of the truck. I guess that's what made the session so exciting for him, knowing that he could be seen by the public. "Oh gosh, there's a man in drag, wrapped in plastic, lying in the back of the truck next to us." Maybe they thought he was dead...

On another occasion he came in and, as usual, was wrapped up. The lady in charge of this session drove him to a hotel. She stood him up, and he was able to shuffle his way along, all the way to the *freight elevator.* She just left him there for a couple of hours. The public probably didn't see him, but the employees must have. It turned out that that was perfectly okay with the hotel managers. They knew all about the Castle, and antics such as this one happened all the time...

The Hothouse Cucumber Guy

By the time this client came in, I had been working for a few years and nothing, I mean nothing, phased me anymore. I was also at a different dungeon where there were really no rules. This place of business had its own supply of dildos, butt plugs, enemas, and condoms, all of which we weren't supposed to be using. Anyhow, this man brought something with him in a plastic bag. He was about five feet eight, fat, and needed a shower. I could smell him when he first walked in the door, and I knew the odor would only get worse if he took off his clothes. My curiosity as to what was in the bag got the better of me, so I agreed to interview him. He called himself "Mr. Martin" and spoke with an accent that sounded Middle-Eastern.

His English wasn't that good either, but that wasn't a problem because he made it very clear what he wanted. We stepped into an empty room to talk, and I asked him what he wanted to do. He looked at me and said very simply, "You are nurse. I have problem in here." (He pointed to his abdomen). "You do examination. You find what problem is." At this point he took a hothouse cucumber out of the plastic bag and handed it to me. "You use this." Earlier in my "career" I would have thought, "Oh, God, no" and referred him to another lady, but by this time I had a "Oh, what the hell" attitude. By the way, the patient/nurse role play is a common one and I had my own little white uniform which I kept in my locker at the dungeon. I also had the shoes, those comfy white nurse's shoes. At least I'd get a break from wearing Darlene's usual four inch heels. We walked to the front desk together and signed up for one hour in the "medical room."

This dungeon didn't really look like a dungeon at all. It was furnished to look like a doctor's office. There was a very old examining table complete with stirrups. Lots of medical gadgets, bottles of fluids like rubbing alcohol, boxes of latex gloves, and containers of cotton balls had been placed on tables. There were also charts of various body parts, (breasts, penises, and vaginas), taped to the walls. We entered the room and I pushed the button on the intercom. I was now "Nurse Darlene" and our session had begun.

"Mr. Martin, I'm Darlene and I'll be your nurse today. I understand you're having some pain in your abdomen. I've had a lot of experience with cases such as yours, and I'm certain I can help you. I need to do a brief examination. Please remove your clothing and lie on the examining table on your stomach."

He did as I instructed. I was right. The odor was even worse. I decided I was going to make this exam *very* brief.

I put on a latex glove and rubbed some lubricant on it. I also smeared some around the entrance to his asshole. I inserted one, then two fingers. I was trying to get him ready for his weapon of choice, the cucumber.

"Mr. Martin, I don't detect any obstruction near the entrance. I need to do a more in-depth examination. Would that be all right with you?"

"Yes, nurse."

"Mr. Martin, for this part of the examination, I think it would be easier if you were on all fours."

He complied.

I started to prepare the cucumber by putting a condom over it, but Mr. Martin objected.

"No, no. The plastic is okay."

As you may know, hothouse cucumbers come wrapped in plastic, but the plastic isn't smooth. It has *ridges* in it. The ridges could tear the lining of the rectum. But, oh well, not my problem.

I positioned a little stool at the end of the table. I had to stand on something because this guy's ass was now over five feet in the air, and I'm not very tall.

"Now Mr. Martin, I'd like you to relax and I'll try to be as gentle as possible."

"Yes, nurse."

So there I was with my face no more than a couple of feet from you-know-what, and the smell was getting *really* bad. I wanted this to be over.

I put the end of the vegetable at the "entrance" and started to push. I was trying to be very careful because I was no kind of nurse and I hadn't done this a lot. To my surprise (and relief), the cucumber slid right in. Well, about three inches of it anyway.

"Very good, Mr. Martin. How are you doing?"

He just made some grunting noises accompanied by nodding which told me grunting was a good thing.

"Mr. Martin, I need to examine more of the interior." I resumed putting pressure in what I hoped was the right direction. Apparently it was, and a few more inches of the "tool" disappeared. I started thinking two things: Either rectums are a lot bigger than I thought, or Mr. Martin has had this exam performed lots of times. It was almost as if he were *sucking* the cucumber inside of himself. Weird.

Several more minutes and several inches later, I was faced with a potential problem. I only had about two inches of the cucumber left. The thing must have been fifteen or so inches long, and I had *two* inches to hang on to. Keep in mind that this wasn't a butt plug. It was tapered at the end. I dug my fingers into the end of it. I mean if I lost this thing inside him, how would I ever pull it out?

And the *smell*. I wanted this session to end. I wanted some fresh air.

Fortunately, a solution to the problem arose. Literally.

Mr. Martin had an erection.

"Mr. Martin, I've located the source of the pain, and I know what to do, but I need your help."

I moved a bottle of oil and a towel within his reach. He began doing his part, while I "assisted" by giving the cucumber gentle thrusts.

He came within a minute, and I thought the gods were smiling on me; that is, until I started to pull the cucumber out.

I had *never* in my life -- I mean it was *awful*. The thing was *covered* with feces and the *smell*. I thought it couldn't get any worse, but it had.

I said to myself, "Hang on Darlene. Don't throw up in front of this guy. You *can't* do *that*."

I dropped the cucumber into the plastic bag the client had brought with him as quickly as I could. I rolled it up and took it to the farthest corner of the room. I was still completely dressed in my little white nurse's uniform, so I was ready to get out of there, but this guy had to get dressed again. The next few minutes seemed like half an hour.

We left the room together and I walked with him to the front desk, the usual protocol. But wait a minute. Before we left the room, he didn't give me anything. He paid the desk person, and still didn't give me anything. He turned around and walked out the front door of the building without giving me ANYTHING. NO TIP! That GOD-AWFUL session and NO TIP! Occasionally, a client didn't tip, but for a session like THIS ONE? I couldn't f---ing believe it.

On top of this, I still had to go back and clean the room. I had to go back to where that *thing* was still rolled up in the corner. I took a deep breath and held it as I went in, grabbed it, ran outside the back door to the dumpster, and threw the damn thing in there. Then I took a long breath of *fresh* air and vowed that I would never, ever, do a session like this one again.

Epilogue

It's clear that one of the things that attracted me to this business was the power and control Darlene had that I never had. My brother was in charge of almost everything I did, and now it was my turn to get even. When I started working, I was aware of a feeling of anger toward all men, just because they were men. In an interview at a dungeon, I'd listen attentively to what the client wanted, smile sweetly, and nod often to indicate I *really* understood. I wanted the man to think I liked him.

That was crap. I was an actress playing a part. He was with Darlene, not *me*. My goal was to give a good performance, which meant that I would allow this guy to look at me. He could look, listen to my voice, and drool. I wanted him to *ache* to touch me. And I would coolly observe him and think, "You fool, you idiot. You will never touch me." Oh, he could attach equipment and spank me, but he wasn't allowed to touch any private parts. More importantly though, he would never touch me emotionally. I would sail through the show and feel nothing. I took pride in being immune. And when he'd put cash in my hand -- that was the best part. His time was over. He had to leave, but I still had his money. The joke was on him.

As the years passed, I became more and more desensitized to human feelings, and my anger morphed into plain old disgust. I saw all men as clients. In normal daily life, men would try to engage me in conversation, and the voice that came out of my mouth was Darlene's.

I'd think, "I wonder what this guy's into. Does he want his cock and balls tied up with rope or clothespins attached to his nipples? Maybe he's more of a masochist and would prefer alligator clamps to clothespins. Or maybe he's more of an exhibitionist and wants to be paraded around the lounge, nude of course." I'd size up every man I saw, anywhere. In the grocery store. Even at school.

School. Most of my students were adults, and even though they saw me as Ms. ______, the teacher, in my mind it felt like the men were looking at Darlene. A male student might be sitting at my desk asking for help with algebra, and I'd think, "Yeah, sure. I know what's really going on in your head." (Pun intended)

During this time I had almost no personal life. I'd go to dinner with someone on rare occasion, but I was just going through the motions. I was Darlene and in my own little world. I couldn't connect with anyone, probably because I didn't really want to. It was safer to play Darlene and not feel part of the real world. Safer. Safety. After a childhood of never feeling safe, it made perfect sense to me that given a list of alternatives, I'd always choose the safest one -- the safest neighborhood in which to live, the safest building, the safest location within the building. Also, the safest job. As long as I was Darlene, I was completely safe from any real human emotion.

I liked this safety thing. Because of my upbringing, depression and anxiety were constant problems. I felt I had to hide inside Darlene to keep myself from falling apart, and for many years it worked quite well for me.

Eventually though, feelings started creeping in. The anger, which had turned into disgust, was becoming empathy. Empathy? Yes, really. The men who came to see Darlene *needed* to see her. They needed to be understood by her and needed the experience she could provide. They were broken people, and I was really helping them get through life. What I finally realized was that I was playing Darlene because I was broken too, and they were helping *me*. I had always been in the same boat as my clients.

It was the spring of 2007. After eighteen years, several strip clubs and dungeons, and five thousand plus sessions, I was back at the dungeon where I had started, and I no longer needed to keep up the charade. I finally had it figured out -- how I could put the two sides of myself together and it would be okay. I had been too lonely for too long and couldn't wait to go out into the real world, connect with someone, and live a real life. Interestingly enough, my epiphany coincided with the owner's decision to retire. It was time to retire Darlene.

Since then, I've been dating, whatever that is. I still don't know what I'm doing, but I'm determined to find the right man to share my life -- a man with whom I can share Ms. ______ the English teacher and Darlene, from Darlene the sex kitten to Darlene the mistress holding the black leather riding crop. He won't judge me or wish that my past had been any different. He'll love the woman Darlene had helped me become and understand that all of it had been necessary. And now it would be his turn to be the recipient, the only recipient, of what I'd learned along the way.

About Darlene...

Darlene was born in Hollywood, California, and grew up in Pasadena, a quiet suburb near Los Angeles. She received a BA in German from California State University, Los Angeles.

For several years she worked in television and film. Credits include *General Hospital*, *Chicken Soup for the Soul*, and the female lead in the film *Monstrosity* in which she played a spaced-out punk rocker. She even photo-doubled for Christian Bale in *Empire of the Sun* and Corey Feldman in *Friday the 13th: A New Beginning* (when they were 14 and 12 respectively). For the past

20 years, she has been a public school teacher in Los Angeles County.

She currently lives in the San Fernando Valley, where she can be found indulging in her favorite hobby, ballroom and country-western dancing.

Her next book is scheduled to be released in early 2013.

For more information on Darlene, please visit her author webpage at www.chancespress.com.

You may also email her at darlene@chancespress.com.